LOUIS FIDGE

essential
English

Book 2

STANLEY
THORNES

Acknowledgements

The author and publishers wish to thank the following
for permission to use copyright material.

Togg and Leftover, Mike Ratnett and June Goulding,
HarperCollins Publishers.

Grace and Family, Mary Hoffman and Caroline Birch,
Frances Lincoln Publishers.

Something Nasty in the Kitchen, Michael Bond,
HarperCollins Publishers.

The Enormous Crocodile, Murray Pollinger Literary Agency
on behalf of Roald Dahl, Jonathan Cape and Penguin Books.

First published in 1996 by
Stanley Thornes (Publishers) Ltd
Ellenborough House
Wellington Street
Cheltenham GL50 1YW

97 98 99 00 / 10 9 8 7 6 5 4 3 2

A catalogue record for this book is available from the British Library.

ISBN 0 7487 2539 3

Design and typesetting by Brian Green Associates.
Illustration by Sue Woollattt, Natalie Bould, Tony Dover, Margaret Theakston,
Claire James and Greg Gormley.

Printed in Hong Kong.

CONTENTS

Who's the strongest?

One morning the North Wind and the Sun saw a horseman wearing a new cloak.

"That young man looks pleased with his new cloak," said the North Wind. "I bet I could easily blow it off his back if I wanted to."

"I don't think you could," said the Sun. "But let us both try to get his coat off. You can try first."

The North Wind began to blow, and blow, and blow. He blew so hard that people had to chase after their hats, leaves were blown from trees and some ships in the harbour were sunk. He blew so hard that all the animals were frightened. The North Wind blew with all his might, but it was no use. As he blew harder, the horseman just pulled his cloak more tightly around himself to keep warm.

Next it was the Sun's turn. He began, gently, to give out his heat. As he did so insects hummed and flowers opened. Birds began to sing. Animals became drowsy and lay down to sleep. With the warmth of the Sun's rays, people came out to gossip. The horseman began to feel very hot, and when he came to the river he took off his clothes and went for a swim.

Aesop's fable

COMPREHENSION

● Starting points ●

Write the answers to these questions in your book.

1 At what time of day did the story take place?

2 Who tried to get the man to take off his cloak first?

3 What happened when the North Wind blew?

4 Why did the man go for a swim?

● Moving on ●

Now, answer these questions in your book.

1 Where do you think the horseman was going? Why do you think this?

2 Who do you think was cleverer - the North Wind or the Sun? Why do you think this?

3 What do you think the moral of the story is?

A **moral** is a lesson we can learn from a story.

STUDY SKILLS

● Placing things in order ●

Write out each of these sets of words in order of size, with the smallest item first.

1 minute hour second week day

2 sentence letter paragraph chapter word

3 cat spider rat horse sheep

4 village house town street city

● Wind speeds ●

Match up each type of wind with the correct description. Write out the chart correctly in your book.

The different wind speeds are in order, but their descriptions have been mixed up.

1 calm	leaves move on the trees
2 gentle breeze	wind is so strong it's difficult to walk
3 strong wind	no wind at all
4 gale	large branches sway on the trees
5 storm	everything in its path is flattened
6 hurricane	trees are blown down

WORD STUDY

● 'ow' and 'ou' words ●

*Use '**ow**' or '**ou**' to fill in the gaps in these words.*
Write the completed words in your book.

1 bl _ _   **2** r _ _ nd   **3** fl _ _   **4** ab _ _ t

5 l _ _ d   **6** gr _ _   **7** cr _ _   **8** s _ _ nd

*Now, use some of the '**ow**' and '**ou**' words to complete*
these sentences. Write the completed sentences in your book.

1 My house is _____ one kilometre away.

2 The wind began to _____.

3 When the beavers built a dam, it stopped the
river's _____.

4 The _____ noise made me jump.

5 The monster had two large _____ eyes.

● 'oa' words ●

*There are eight '**oa**'
words in my cloak.
Find them and write
them in your book.*

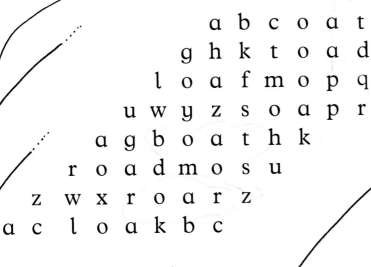

LANGUAGE STUDY

● Adjectives ●

Copy these sentences into your book. Underline the **adjectives** *in each one.*

1 The wild dog bit my left leg.

2 The strong man carried the heavy box.

3 The funny clown fell into a bath of cold water.

4 The beautiful, yellow rose won the first prize.

5 I crashed into the huge rock and scratched my new bike.

Adjectives
are describing words. They tell you more about **nouns**.

extra

Think of a suitable **noun** *to go with each* **adjective**:

1 a cold _____

2 a dark _____

3 a prickly ____

4 a wobbly ____

5 a funny _____

● Opposites ●

The man is **strong** but the boy is **weak**.

The words 'strong' and 'weak' have opposite meanings.

Fill in the gaps with suitable **opposites**. *Write out the completed sentences in your book.*

1 The coffee was **hot** but the tea was _____.

2 The red door was **open** but the green door was ____.

3 In the morning it is **light** but at night it is _____.

4 Lead is **heavy** but a feather is _____.

5 My cloak is **new** but my trousers are _____.

6 This stone feels **smooth** but this wood feels _____.

7

WRITING WORKSHOP

● Full stops and capital letters ●

Rewrite the pairs of sentences below in your book. Add capital letters and full stops in the correct places.

1 the man was too hot he took off his cloak

2 he put it on the grass after this he went for a swim in the river

3 a beggar saw the cloak on the grass he picked it up and ran off with it

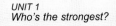

I have missed out the full stops and capital letters from these sentences. Help me to put them right.

● Questions and answers ●

In your book, write out suitable questions for these answers. Don't forget to write a question mark at the end of each one. The first one has been done for you.

1 **Question**: *Why did the man take his cloak off?*
   Answer: He took it off because he was too hot.

2 **Question**:
   Answer: He went for a swim in the river.

3 **Question**:
   Answer: It was on the grass.

4 **Question**:
   Answer: He picked it up and ran off with it.

● The storm ●

Look at the picture carefully. Write two or three sentences which say what you think happened next.

● What happened next? ●

Read the story below. Write two or three sentences that say what you think happened next.

Tom and Tess rowed the boat out on to the lake. Suddenly a storm blew up. The boat was tossed about by the waves.

● A mixed-up story ●

The sentences in this story have been mixed up. Write them out in the correct order in your book.

They ran into the sea, laughing and splashing each other.

It was a lovely, sunny day.

They did not notice that they had left their clothes very near to the water.

Tom and Tess put on their swimming costumes.

extra

Make up a good ending for this story. Write it in your book. Give your story a title.

9

Togg's egg

TOGG was a caveman. He lived all alone in his cave, deep in a valley. One morning Togg was clearing out the back of his cave when he found a huge egg. 'This will make a wonderful breakfast,' he thought. 'I will invite all my friends to share it.' He rolled the egg out into the warm sunshine and set off over the hills to find everyone.

The day grew hotter and hotter. As the sun beat down on the egg, weird things began to happen. There was a strange tapping sound and the huge egg wobbled and shook. Then 'CRAAAAACK!' the shell split open.

When Togg and his friends returned, all that was left of the enormous egg were huge, broken pieces of shell. "We're too late," said Flowulf. "Somebody must have eaten it," mumbled Coppertop. "Fancy leaving it around like that!" said Redbeard. And they turned right round and set off home again, feeling very disappointed and hungry. Togg was so upset about his egg that he went straight to bed and stayed there for the rest of the day. 'I wonder what happened to it?' he thought.

Togg's friends had not gone very far, when suddenly an enormous monster leapt out at them. "Boo!" it shouted. "Help!" shrieked the cave people, and they ran to hide. Everything went quiet. "It's gone," whispered Redbeard, and they all crept out. But the huge monster was waiting. "Blaaah!" it went, jumping at them again. Togg's friends fled home as fast as they could.

Mike Ratnett and June Goulding

COMPREHENSION

● Starting points ●

1 Togg lived in a
   a) hut   **b)** cave   **c)** pit

2 Togg thought that he would eat the egg for
   a) breakfast   **b)** lunch   **c)** tea

3 The eggshell
   a) turned blue   **b)** split open   **c)** disappeared

4 When the monster first saw Togg's friends, it shouted
   a) 'Gotcha!'   **b)** 'Blaaah!'   **c)** 'Boo!'

● Moving on ●

1 Write a list of some of the things Togg might have had in his cave.

2 What sort of person do you think Togg was? Write a description of him in your book.

3 Write some sentences which say what you think happened next.

Choose the right answers. Write them in your book.

STUDY SKILLS

● Alphabetical order ●

Write these words in your book in alphabetical order, according to their first letters.

1 monster   cave   egg   friend

2 bed   moon   star   cloud

3 jump   run   sit   hop

Now write these words in order, according to the second letters.

1 bucket   bell   banana   bird

2 cave   crisp   clog   cheese

3 fog   floor   fry   fast

i We need to know about **alphabetical order** to use dictionaries and encyclopedias.

i When you put words that begin with the same letter in **alphabetical order**, you must look at the second letter of each word.

11

WORD STUDY

● Root words ●

What's that **tap**ping sound?

Tap! Tap!

Sometimes longer words come from shorter words. We call the shorter ones **root words**.

The word '**tap**ping' comes from the **root** word '**tap**'.

*Write these words in your book. Underline the **root word** in each, like this:* <u>tap</u>ping.

1 hotter	**2** lumpy	**3** homeless	**4** pictured
5 wooden	**6** unhappy	**7** baker	**8** shrieked
9 wonderful	**10** dangerous		

● Three-letter patterns ●

Copy this word grid carefully into your book. Use some coloured pencils to underline:

- the '**scr**' words in **red**
- the '**str**' words in **green**
- the '**spl**' words in **yellow**
- the '**spr**' words in **blue**

split	scrap	string
strip	spring	scream
splash	stream	sprint
strong	scrub	sprout

extra

Try to think of one more word that begins with each of the letter patterns.

LANGUAGE STUDY

● Proper nouns ●

Hello! My name is Togg.

I'm called Redbeard.

> **i** Special names of: people, places or things are called **proper nouns**. They begin with a **capital letter**.

*Copy the page below into your book. Fill in the spaces with suitable **proper nouns**.*

My name:
My school:
My address:
My birth month:
My favourite day of the week:
Name of a country:
Name of a river:
Name of a character from television:

> **i** **Common** (or ordinary) **nouns** are the names of people, places or things in general.

● Common (or ordinary) nouns ●

*Copy these sentences into your book. Underline all the **common nouns**. The first one has been done for you.*

1 In the <u>valley</u> there was a <u>cave</u>.

2 The egg was huge and had a hard shell.

3 A monster frightened the cave people.

4 The plums were in a plastic bag.

5 The farmer sold some of his cows.

6 Some children climbed up the hill.

> **extra**
>
> Finish each sentence with a **common noun**. Write the sentences in your book.
>
> **1** Thursday is a **<u>day</u>**.
>
> **2** March is a ____.
>
> **3** Mars is a ____.
>
> **4** The Thames is a _____.
>
> **5** Everest is a _____.
>
> **6** Glasgow is a _____.

13

WRITING WORKSHOP

● Joining sentences ●

1 Togg got up. He got dressed.
Togg got up and got dressed.

> *Join each pair of sentences with 'and' to make one longer sentence. The first one has been done for you.*

2 The woman got out a chair. She sat down.

3 The door opened. An old lady came out.

4 I turned on the hose. Then I watered the flowers.

*Now, join these pairs of sentences using '**but**'.*

1 Tom wrote ten answers. Five were wrong.

2 The monster looked frightening. It was really very friendly.

3 Togg played football. He didn't score any goals.

4 We looked around the shops. I got lost.

● Shortening long sentences ●

Rewrite each long sentence, making it into two or more shorter sentences. Do it like this:

The monster ran after me and gave me a hug.
The monster ran after me. It gave me a hug.

1 The monster hid behind the rock and jumped out on Togg.

2 I went to a party and had a lot to eat and played some good games.

3 I keep my pet mouse in a cage but sometimes it gets out and then my mum gets cross.

4 At school Tom did some reading and then painting but when he did maths he got a lot of sums wrong.

> **i** Check that you have added **capital letters** and **full stops** to all the sentences in the correct places.

14

● The party ●

Write a letter to reply to this invitation.

The Cave
Giant's Hill
Cropton
WA1 8GH

5th May

Dear friend,
I am having a party at my cave on Saturday, from 4pm until 10pm. We will be having a special meal to celebrate Monster's birthday. I have enclosed a menu for you to look at. I hope you can come. Please write and let me know.

From,
Togg.

Monster Menu

Starters
Melon or garlic bread

Main course
Pizza or a hamburger with French fries

Dessert
Ice cream or apple pie

Drinks
Cola or fruit juice

Choose what you would like to eat and drink from the menu. In your book, draw a menu and list your choices on it. Draw pictures of the foods you have listed and decorate the menu.

extra

1 Imagine that you are having a party. Write an invitation letter to one of your friends.

2 Make up a menu that has your favourite foods on it.

3 Imagine that one of your uncles or aunts has sent you something you really wanted for your birthday. Write a thank you letter.

15

Who landed on the Moon first?

A RUSSIAN spaceship called Lunar 2 was the first spacecraft to reach the Moon. It crash-landed on the Moon's surface. Soon after this, the Americans began to plan how they would build a spacecraft that could carry astronauts to the Moon. The race to put the first person on the moon had begun!

By 1969, the scientists of America were ready. The whole world watched with wonder as three astronauts travelled to the Moon in the Apollo 11 spacecraft. This was launched from Earth by a giant Saturn rocket. It took four days to reach the Moon. The main spacecraft continued to fly around the Moon while two of the astronauts, Neil Armstrong and Edwin 'Buzz' Aldrin, flew down to the planet's surface in a small landing-craft. Millions of television viewers heard the words 'The eagle has landed!' as the landing-craft touched down. On July 20th 1969, the first men set foot on the Moon.

Moon facts

▶ The Moon is nearly 400,000km from Earth.

▶ The Moon has no atmosphere.

▶ One day on the Moon lasts nearly 30 Earth days.

▶ It can be as hot as 100°C and as cold as -170°C.

COMPREHENSION

● Starting points ●

1 The first spacecraft to reach the Moon was American.

2 Apollo 11 was a Russian spacecraft.

3 Only two astronauts actually walked on the Moon in July 1969.

4 The Moon is over 400,000km from Earth.

5 One day on the Moon is a lot longer than one day on Earth.

*Read these sentences carefully. Write whether they are **true** or **false** in your book.*

● Moving on ●

Write the answers to these questions in your book.

1 Why do you think there was a race to get the first person on the Moon?

2 Why do you think the astronauts had to wear special space-suits to walk on the Moon?

3 What do you think the words 'The eagle has landed!' meant?

STUDY SKILLS

● Crossword clues ●

In your book, write some suitable clues for this crossword.

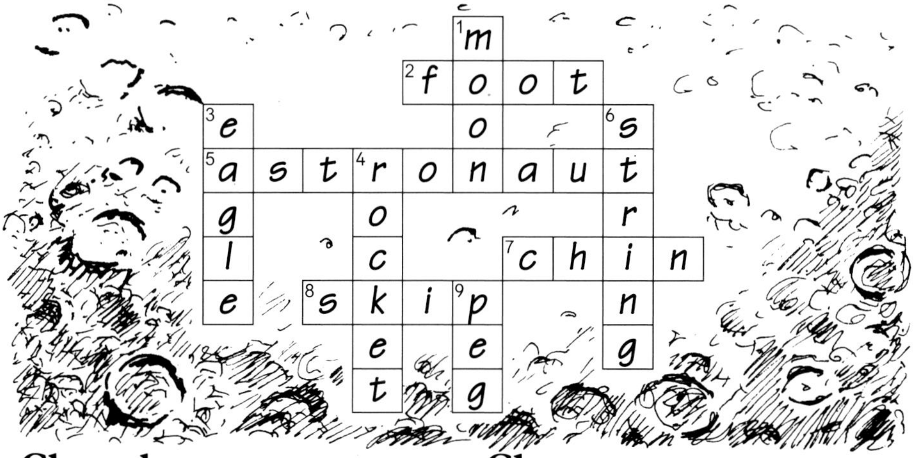

Clues down	Clues across
1 _____	2 _____
3 _____	5 *Someone who travels in a spacecraft.*
4 _____	7 _____
6 _____	8 _____
9 _____	

extra

Write a description of how you think Neil Armstrong and Edwin Aldrin felt when they stepped out on to the Moon.

extra

Look up the meanings of these words in a dictionary. Write them in your book.

*Words:
orbit
atmosphere
launch
gravity*

WORD STUDY

● 'age' and 'ace' words ●

*Complete these words using either **'ace'** or **'age'**. Write them in your book.*

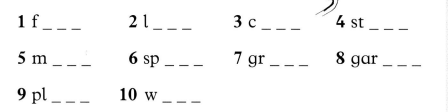

We live in a space age.

1 f _ _ _ **2** l _ _ _ **3** c _ _ _ **4** st _ _ _

5 m _ _ _ **6** sp _ _ _ **7** gr _ _ _ **8** gar _ _ _

9 pl _ _ _ **10** w _ _ _

Write which of the words above means:

a) somewhere you put a pet bird

b) somewhere you keep a car

c) something you get paid for working

d) the place where actors act

e) rockets fly into this

Say the words **'ace'** and **'age'**. Listen to the sounds that the **'c'** and **'g'** make. They have soft sounds. The **'c'** sounds like **'s'**. The **'g'** sounds like **'j'**.

● Jumbled letters - 'ew' words ●

*Unscramble the letters in these **'ew'** words. Use the clues to help you. Write them in your book like this:*

lewf - moved like a bird = flew

1 enw   not old

2 wef   not many

3 regw   got bigger

4 wehc   to eat something tough

5 wets   like a thick soup

6 rescw   used to join bits of wood together

extra

*In your book, write down any other **'ew'** words you can think of.*

18

LANGUAGE STUDY

● Verbs ●

We <u>flew</u> to the Moon.

Our spacecraft <u>landed</u> on the Moon.

Most verbs are doing words.

extra

*In your book, write as many **verbs** as you can that say what each of these people might do. For example:*

1 A skater **glides**, **slides**, **slips**, **falls**, **jumps**.

2 A footballer...

3 A builder...

4 A teacher...

*Copy these sentences into your book. Choose the best **verb** from the brackets to complete each one.*

1 The eagle (flew, glided, swooped) down on to the mouse.

2 The mouse (walked, wriggled, scampered) back to its home.

3 The band (played, made, blew) some loud music.

4 The old man (walked, skipped, plodded) up the hill.

5 The butterfly (hovered, sank, climbed) near to the flowers.

6 The car (hopped, skidded, stopped) on the ice.

● The verb 'to be' ●

*In each of these sentences there is a **verb** which is part of the **verb 'to be'**. Copy the sentences and underline the **verb** in each. The first one has been done for you.*

1 The Romans <u>were</u> brave soldiers.

2 Ranjit is a great singer.

3 Our teacher was late this morning.

4 I am good at spelling.

5 Henry VIII was a famous king.

6 An apple is a kind of fruit.

I <u>am</u> an astronaut.

19

WRITING WORKSHOP

● Sentences make sense ●

*There are **phrases** and **proper sentences** in the piece of writing below. Write out the **proper sentences** in your book.*

On the Moon's surface

The spacecraft landed on the Moon.

The astronauts stepped out of the door.

At the top of the hill

During the night

They carried out some tests.

In the sky

The astronauts returned to Earth safely.

Along the road

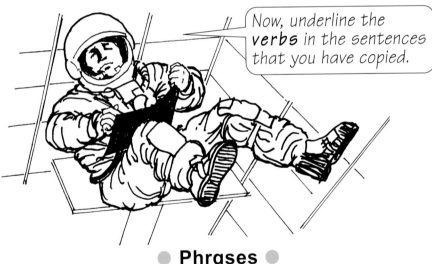

> Now, underline the **verbs** in the sentences that you have copied.

i 1 A **sentence** must make sense.

2 A **sentence** must contain at least one **verb**.

3 A group of words without a **verb** is called a **phrase**.

● Phrases ●

*The **phrases** in the box can be used as the beginnings of sentences. Make up endings for them and write them in your book like this:*

In my pocket I found a five pound note.

In my pocket	In the sky	On the pavement
Behind a tree	At midnight	Under the sea

extra

*Use these phrases **at the end** of some sentences:*

... on the lake.
... on top of the hill.
... in the morning.
... during the storm.
... off the ladder.

20

● Adventure in space ●

Use these pictures to help you to write a story. Make up an exciting ending for it.

1 Remember to say which planet the astronauts go to and what it looks like.

2 Include what the astronauts say to each other as they land on the planet.

3 Write how you think they feel.

When you have finished, read your story.

● Does it make sense?

● Do you want to change anything?

● Check the spelling and punctuation.

21

Do you remember?

STUDY SKILLS

Match up each definition with the correct word from the box. Write the answers in your book.

1 a) You sit on this when you ride a bicycle.

b) You push these with your feet to make the bicycle move.

c) You hold on to these to steer the bicycle.

d) You use these to make the bicycle stop.

e) This is made of rubber and is filled with air.

2 *Write out the different parts of a bicycle (listed in the box) in alphabetical order.*

brakes

tyre

pedals

saddle

handlebars

WORD STUDY

Change the 'o' to an 'e' in the words below. Write the new words in your book.

1 a) now   **b)** crow   **c)** grow   **d)** blow

e) flow   **f)** stow

In your book, write out the pairs of rhyming words.

2

A	**B**
cloak	space
know	page
boat	soak
roast	sound
face	about
stage	boast
round	coat
shout	slow

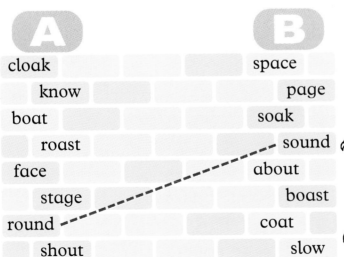

22

LANGUAGE STUDY

1 a) I helped my _____ to peel the _____ for lunch.

b) My birthday is in the month of _____ .

c) The _____ after Sunday is _____ .

d) My favourite _____ is _____ .

e) My teacher's name is ____ _____ .

*Think of a suitable **common noun** to go with each* **adjective**.

2 a) a huge _____   **b)** a tiny _____

c) a noisy _____   **d)** an empty _____

e) a sticky _____   **f)** a sweet _____

*Choose suitable **common** or **proper** **nouns** to complete each sentence. Write the completed sentences in your book.*

WRITING WORKSHOP

1 a) The dog sat under the tree. It went to sleep.
The dog sat under the tree and went to sleep.

*Join each pair of sentences together with '**and**' to make one long sentence.*

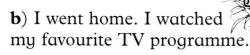

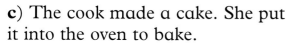

b) I went home. I watched my favourite TV programme.

c) The cook made a cake. She put it into the oven to bake.

d) The girl changed. Then she went out to play.

e) The butterfly fluttered around. It settled on a pink flower.

Make up some sentences that begin with these **phrases**:

2 a) Last night...   **b)** Last year...

c) Under my bed...   **d)** The sound of bells...

GRACE lived with her Ma and her Nana and a cat called Paw-Paw. Next to her family, what Grace liked best were stories. Some she knew and some she made up, and she was particularly interested in ones about fathers because she didn't have one.

"You do too have a father," her Ma said, when she caught Grace talking that way. "I must have told you a hundred times about how we split up and your Papa went back to Africa. He has another family now, but he's still your father even though he doesn't live with us any more."

In her school reading books Grace saw that all families had a mother and a father, a boy and a girl, and a dog and a cat. "Our family's not right," she told Nana. "We need a father and a brother and a dog."

"Well," said Nana, "I'm not sure how Paw-Paw would feel about a dog. And what about me? Are there any Nanas in your school book?"

Grace shook her head. "So do you want me to go?" asked Nana, smiling.

"Of course not!" Grace said, hugging her.

Nana hugged her back. "Families are what you make them," she said.

Mary Hoffman and Caroline Binch

> *Read the story again, then finish these sentences with sensible endings. Write them in your book.*

COMPREHENSION

● Starting points ●

1 Grace lived with...

2 Grace's father lived in...

3 When Nana asked Grace if she wanted her to go, Grace said...

4 Nana told Grace, 'Families are what...'

● Moving on ●

1 How do you know that Grace missed her father?

2 What sort of a person do you think Nana was? Why do you think this?

3 What did Nana mean when she said, 'Families are what you make them?'

> Here's the **contents page** of a **non-fiction** book I borrowed from the library. The **contents page** tells you what's in the book.

STUDY SKILLS

● Using a contents page ●

Contents

*Use the **contents page** to answer these questions. Write the answers in your book.*

1 Which part of the book would you turn to to find out about:

   a) cavemen?   **b**) what is needed to build a house?

   c) houses in India?   **d**) living on the Moon?

2 What sort of information would you expect to find on pages 7-10?

3 If you needed to find out the name of a rabbit's home, where would you look?

> ⓘ We can divide books into two types - **fiction and non-fiction**.
>
> **Fiction** books do not have to be about real or true things. They may be about imaginary people and adventures. Most story books are **fiction**.
>
> **Non-fiction** books are about real things and real people. We use them to find out information.

WORD STUDY

● Word families ●

Sort the words in the box into three word families.

Write them in your book like this:

'or' words	'aw' words	'au' words
fork		

fork
launch
paw
saw
torn
autumn
straw
claw
sport
saucer
pause

extra

Add some more words to each family.

● 'oi' and 'oy' words ●

Choose either '**oi**' or '**oy**' to fill in the gaps. Write the completed words in your book.

1 b _ _   2 b _ _ l   3 j _ _ n   4 t _ _   5 p _ _ nt

6 destr _ _   7 enj _ _   8 n _ _ se   9 ann _ _   10 av _ _ d

Write the words in your book which mean:

a) to make water very hot

b) the sharp end of a pencil

c) to break up and spoil

d) the opposite of girl

e) something you play with

f) to make someone mad

extra

How many words can you think of that rhyme with '**oil**'? Write them in your book.

LANGUAGE STUDY

● Adverbs ●

"I miss my father,"
Grace said <u>sadly</u>.

> An **adverb** is a word that tells you more about a verb, e.g. I ran **quickly**.

Add 'ly' to the words in the box to make them into **adverbs**. *Use these* **adverbs** *to complete the sentences below. Write the sentences in your book.*

1 I heard the band playing very _____ .

2 The moon shone _____ .

3 The girl spoke _____ to her mum.

4 It is _____ five o'clock.

5 _____ there was a loud bang.

sudden
bright
loud
near
rude

● Shortening words ●

> I'd love to see my father again.

Match the **shortened words** *from Set A to their longer forms in Set B. Write them in your book like this:*

didn't = did not.

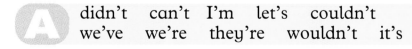

A didn't   can't   I'm   let's   couldn't
we've   we're   they're   wouldn't   it's

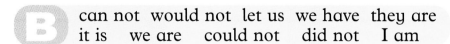

B can not would not let us we have they are
it is   we are   could not   did not   I am

> Sometimes when we join two words together, some letters are missed out. We use an **apostrophe** (like this ') to show where the missing letters used to be, e.g. I'll = I will.

WRITING WORKSHOP

● Punctuating a passage ●

*Rewrite this passage about Grace in your book. Divide it into sentences. Write in the missing **punctuation marks**.*

grace lived in england with her family she had
a cat called paw-paw grace hadnt seen her
father since she was small he lived in africa
grace wasnt very happy because she missed her
father very much she couldnt even remember
what he looked like grace hoped that she would
see him one day

● List poems ●

Copy out this poem in your best handwriting and decorate it.

> **List poems** don't have to **rhyme**.

In this country there's a town.
In the town there's a street.
In that street there's a house.
In that house there's a bedroom.
In that bedroom a girl is dreaming.

Now, make up a list poem of things you like to dream about (or don't like to dream about!). Write it out like this:

I like to dream...
  I like to dream about summer holidays by the sea.
  I like to dream about delicious food and ice cream.

> **extra**
> Make up a list poem called '**A good friend**'. Start the poem like this: A good friend is...

● Describing places ●

When I went to Africa, things were so different. I liked the market best.

On the next day they went to the food market. It was much more exciting than shopping at home. Even the money had crocodiles on it! Lots of women carried their shopping on their heads. Then they went to a stall which was like stepping inside a rainbow. There was cloth with crocodiles and elephants on it, and cloth with patterns made from pebbles and shells. And so many colours! "We can choose some cloth for Grace's first African dress," said Papa. Grace and Nana spent a long time choosing. No one was in a hurry.

Mary Hoffman and Caroline Binch

In your book, write a description of a market or shopping centre you know well.

● Describing feelings ●

Write sentences in your book that say how you would feel if....

1 ... you weren't allowed to watch your favourite TV programme.

2 ... you had just won a race on sports day.

3 ... you heard scratching at your window at night.

4 ... you had just come off a big dipper at a funfair.

5 ... you were lost in a busy shopping centre.

Before you start writing, close your eyes and think about the place. What can you hear, see, smell, touch, taste? Use lots of **adjectives** (describing words) to make your piece of writing more interesting.

29

Something nasty in the kitchen

QUITE early in the morning, Paddington had run out of saucepans. It was the first big meal he had ever cooked and he wanted it to be something special.

He'd looked up the chapter on dumplings in Mrs Bird's cookery book, and followed the instructions most carefully: he put in two parts of flour, one of suet, then added milk before stirring the whole lot together. But somehow, instead of the mixture turning into neat balls, as it showed in the picture, it had all gone runny. Then when he'd added more flour and suet, it had gone lumpy instead and stuck to his fur, so that he'd had to add more milk and then more flour and suet, until he had a huge mountain of dumpling mixture in the middle of the kitchen table. He wiped his paws carefully on Mrs Bird's apron and, after looking around for a large enough bowl, scraped the dumpling mixture into his hat.

Michael Bond

COMPREHENSION

● Starting points ●

Read these sentences and think of a good word to go in each space. Write the words in your book like this:
1) morning.

One ___1___ Paddington decided to cook a ___2___ . He had never cooked anything before, so he looked in Mrs Bird's ___3___ book. When Paddington mixed up the ___4___ , he put in some flour, suet and ___5___ . Something had gone wrong because the ___6___ had gone all runny. When he added more flour and suet, it went all ___7___ . Paddington then scraped the mixture off the table and into his ___8___ .

● Moving on ●

1 Paddington made up a special menu for the meal he cooked. Write down some things you think he may have included.

2 What things tell you that Paddington was not used to cooking? Write some of them in your book.

extra

In your book, write a description of what you think the kitchen looked like when Paddington had finished cooking.

STUDY SKILLS

● Cause and effect ●

1 Tom wanted to cook a meal because...

2 Tara dropped the eggs because...

3 Tom cooked the cabbage in the kettle because...

4 Tara got gravy all over her clothes because...

5 The pastry went all lumpy because...

6 The pie burnt because...

We always get in a mess when we cook. Think up some good endings for these sentences and write them in your book.

● Different points of view ●

Tom and Tara loved to go into the kitchen and cook. They thought that if they cooked a meal, it would be a lovely surprise for their mum when she came home from work. They didn't mind the mess or the fact that things didn't go as expected! Tom and Tara didn't seem to think about any of the dangers of cooking without an older person watching them.

Write what you think Tom and Tara's mum said when she got home.

31

WORD STUDY

● 'er', 'ir' and 'ur' words ●

Copy this word grid into your book. Use some coloured pencils to underline:

- *the 'er' words in red*

- *the 'ir' words in blue*

- *the 'ur' words in yellow.*

bird	turn	serve	girl
curl	term	first	hurt
verse	dirt	burn	jerk

● **Compound words** ●

*Match up each word in Box A to a word in Box B, to make some **compound words**. Write the words in your book.*

sauce + pan = saucepan

A foot play car up my
rain cup bed sauce

B pet self bow ball pan
room board ground stairs

extra

Choose one of these letter patterns - 'er', 'ir', or 'ur' - to finish each word in the box. Write the completed words in your book.

st_ _

p_ _ haps

n_ _ rse

sh_ _ t

diff _ _ ent

b_ _ thday

Th_ _ sday

ⓘ 'Saucepan' is a **compound word**. A **compound word** is made from two smaller words joined together, e.g. sauce + pan = saucepan.

LANGUAGE STUDY

● Pronouns ●

*Rewrite this passage, choosing suitable **pronouns** from the box to fill in the gaps. You will need to use some of the **pronouns** more than once.*

Tom was in a mess. ____ had saucepans everywhere. Tom got hold of the last saucepan. ____ filled _____ with water. Next, Tom got some potatoes and peeled ____. Tom cut ____ up and put ____ into the saucepan. Just then, ____ mum came in. "What a mess!" _____ shouted.

> **i** A **pronoun** takes the place of a noun:
> The bag is heavy.
> **It** (the bag) is full of shopping.

it
them
his
she
he

● Noise words ●

Tom's mum heard the sound of **banging** saucepans and **rattling** dishes.

*Think of a suitable **adjective** to describe the sound that each of these things makes. Write the pairs of words in your book.*

1 *flapping* wings
2 _____ raindrops
3 _____ drums
4 _____ coins
5 _____ horns
6 _____ sausages
7 _____ wind
8 _____ doors

*Choose a suitable **verb** that describes the noise each animal makes, e.g. A monkey **chatters**.*

1 A lion _____.
2 A pig _____.
3 A mouse ___.
4 An elephant _____.
5 A wolf _____.

33

WRITING WORKSHOP

● Commas ●

Copy these sentences into your book. Write in the missing **commas**.

1 I like art reading swimming and history.

2 Tom collects stamps coins pencils and stickers.

3 On my desk there is a book a pen a key and a ruler.

4 My favourite fruits are apples grapes bananas and oranges.

> **Commas** are used to separate items in a list, e.g. Paddington cooked some potatoes, cabbage, sprouts and peas. We do not usually write a comma before '**and**'.

> **extra**
>
> *Make a list of four things:*
> ● *you like eating*
> ● *you find in a fridge*
> ● *you would like for your birthday.*

● Shortening words ●

Match the **shortened forms** *of the words in Set A to the longer forms of these words in Set B. Do it like this:*

Rd. = Road.

A Rd. St. Ave. Sq. Gdns.
Pl. Cresc. Bldgs.

B Avenue Gardens Crescent Road
Square Street Place Buildings

> When we shorten words, we call them **abbreviations**. When words are shortened in this way, they are often followed by full stops.

Below are the **abbreviations** *of the names of some of the months of the year. Write them out in full in your book.*

Jan.   Feb.   Mar.   Apr.   Aug.

Sept.   Oct.   Nov.   Dec.

● Acrostic poems ●

*Write an **acrostic poem** for your name.*

P leasant personality

A lways up to something

D angerous bear

D oes try hard

I nterested in everything

N ever a dull moment

G ets into a mess

T rouble is his middle name

O ne of a kind

N ice and cuddly

Here's an **acrostic poem** that I wrote for my name!

extra

Now, write an acrostic poem using one of your friends' names.

● Good table manners ●

Draw a poster which lists some rules for eating properly. Set out your poster like the one shown below.

Give your poster a title.

Draw a suitable picture:

Good table manners

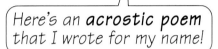

★ Always sit down.
★ Don't talk with your mouth full.

Make up some do's and don'ts:

First of all, draw your poster in rough:
● Try out different ideas.
● Check your spellings.
● Try to keep your writing all the same size.

extra

Make up some rules for the way you should behave:

● *in class*
● *in the playground*
● *in the swimming pool.*

35

Life in Ancient Egypt Unit 6

1   Work

EGYPTIAN women did not go out to work. They stayed at home and worked there. Most ordinary Egyptian men had two jobs. They worked on the land when it was not flooded by the River Nile. When the water in the River Nile did get too high and flood, the farmers did other jobs. Some were builders or fishermen. Others were artists or jewellers. The priests and other important people did not do any farming.

2   _____

THE weather in Egypt was very hot, so people did not wear many clothes. Men, women and children wore either thin-cloth kilts or simple robes. On their feet, people wore open sandals. Men and women shaved off their hair, to keep cool. They wore wigs when they dressed for special occasions.

3   _____

CHILDREN in Egypt grew up to do the same jobs as their parents. Girls stayed at home with their mothers. They learned to look after the house and to cook. Boys went to work with their fathers and learned to do their jobs. They didn't go to school unless they had to learn to write, to become scribes.

COMPREHENSION

● Starting points ●

1 Egyptian women...

2 Egyptian men worked...

3 To keep cool, people shaved...

4 Girls learned to...

5 Boys only went to school if...

Think of a suitable ending for each sentence.

● Moving on ●

1 Write some of the ways in which the lives of Egyptian men and women were different.

2 Would you like to shave your head in hot weather? Write some reasons for your answer.

3 How do you think we know so much about life in Egypt so long ago?

STUDY SKILLS

● Main ideas ●

*The first **paragraph**, on page 36, tells you all about the jobs we do.*

*This is the **main idea** of the paragraph, which is why we have given it the heading '**Work**'.*

The information on page 36 has been divided into three **paragraphs**. A **paragraph** is a group of sentences which usually has one main idea. When we write in **paragraphs**, we start each one on a new line.

*Read the other **paragraphs** again carefully. What is the **main idea** of each **paragraph**? Think up a good heading for each of them. Write the headings in your book.*

● Paragraphs ●

*Write a **paragraph** about each of the things below. Each **paragraph** should be three or more sentences long and should be given a suitable title.*

1 What you like about television

2 Your favourite foods

3 An adult you know well

WORD STUDY

● Codes ●

a	b	c	d	e	f	g	h	i	j	k	l	m
1	2	3	4	5	6	7	8	9	10	11	12	13

n	o	p	q	r	s	t	u	v	w	x	y	z
14	15	16	17	18	19	20	21	22	23	24	25	26

Use the code to work out what words are written below.
Write them in your book, like this: 3 1 14
                                          c a n

1 | 3 | 1 | 14 | 2 | 23 | 1 | 14 | 20 |

3 | 19 | 1 | 9 | 4 | 4 | 3 | 15 | 21 | 12 | 4 |

5 | 2 | 5 | 3 | 1 | 21 | 19 | 5 |

Now, use the code to work out what this message says.
Write it in your book.

   3   1   14   25 15 21   18 5 1 4

   20 8 9 19   13 5 19 19 1 7 5 ?

extra

In your book, write a message in code for someone else to read.

● Suffixes ●

Copy this grid into your book. Fill in the missing words.

verb	verb + 'ing'	verb + 'ed'
stay	staying	
learn		learned
	working	
talk		talked
	watching	
help		
		fixed
	floating	

 Sometimes we add extra letters to the ends of words to change their meaning. These endings are called **suffixes**. We often add **suffixes** to the ends of **verbs**.

LANGUAGE STUDY

● Past tense ●

*Copy these sentences into your book. Underline the **verb** in each one. The **verbs** are all in the **past tense**.*

1 Egyptians built their houses out of mud bricks.
2 People painted the outside walls white.
3 Egyptian houses had flat roofs.
4 People dried washing on their roofs.
5 Most people cooked outside.

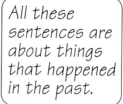

All these sentences are about things that happened in the past.

Some **verbs** tell us about things that happened in the **past**. These **verbs** are written in the **past tense**.

extra

*Write five sentences about things you did yesterday. Underline the **verbs** in each one.*

● Present tense ●

*Copy Tara's sentences into your book. Fill in the gaps with suitable **verbs**. These **verbs** are in the **present tense**.*

We _____ our food in the kitchen. We _____ a lot of food in the fridge.
My mum _____ our clothes in a washing-machine.

When we write about things that are happening now, the **verbs** are written in the **present tense**. There are two ways of writing **verbs** in the **present tense**:

1 Joe **reads** a book.

2 Joe **is reading** a book.

*Now, add '**ing**' to the **verbs** in the box, and use them to finish these sentences. Write the sentences in your book.*

1 Khayyam is ***singing*** loudly.

2 Asif is _____ football.

3 Charlotte is _____ a model pyramid.

4 The sun is _____ brightly.

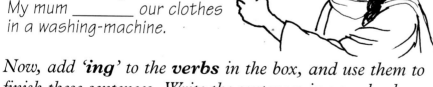

play

sing

make

shine

WRITING WORKSHOP

● Alphabets ●

The Greek alphabet:

ΑΒΓΔΕΖΗΘΙΚΛΜΝΞΟΠΡΣΤΥΦΧΨΩ

The Roman alphabet:

ABCDEFGHIKLMNOPQRSTVXYZ

In your book, write out our alphabet in capital letters.

1 Underline the letters we have added to the Roman alphabet.

2 Ring the vowels.

● Spacing and printing ●

Print these sentences in your book in capitals, leaving spaces between the words.

1 OURALPHABETHASTWENTY-SIXLETTERS.

2 OURALPHABETISMADEUPOFVOWELSAND CONSONANTS.

3 THEEGYPTIANSWROTEINPICTURES.

4 INTHEPASTPEOPLEWROTEWITHFEATHERS.

5 ITISHARDTOREADWORDSWHENTHERE ARENOSPACESBETWEENTHEM.

ⓘ The Greeks invented an alphabet which had 24 letters.

ⓘ The Romans used the Greek alphabet to make their own alphabet. The Roman alphabet had only 23 letters.

ⓘ The Greeks did not leave spaces between words when they wrote sentences!

The Egyptians used different symbols from us when they wrote. They used a sort of picture-writing called **hieroglyphics**. *Find out all you can about this way of writing.*

40

● Types of writing ●

We write for lots of different reasons. Think of at least ten reasons. Write them in your book like this:

To write notes

To tell jokes

To advertise

● People who need to write ●

Why do the people listed below need to be able to read and write? Write some sentences that explain why in your book.

1 A doctor **2** A cook **3** A postman

4 An author **5** A bus driver **6** A traveller

7 A teacher **8** You

41

Do you remember?

STUDY SKILLS

Who do you think said each of these things after the accident? Match each person to the correct statement.

1

People	Things that were said
Driver of the car	I saw it all. It was the driver's fault.
Cyclist	I put the brakes on but my car skidded.
Policeman	I was just crossing the road when I got hit.
Witness	You must have been driving too fast.

WORD STUDY

a	b	o	i	l	c	d	e	f
g	l	a	u	n	c	h	i	j
t	u	r	n	c	l	a	w	k
l	m	n	p	a	u	s	e	o
p	s	t	r	a	w	q	r	s
t	o	y	r	o	y	a	l	t
c	o	i	n	d	i	r	t	y
u	v	t	h	i	r	d	w	x
y	z	a	c	b	u	r	s	t

Find these words in the puzzle and write them in your book:
- two '**aw**' words
- two '**au**' words
- two '**oi**' words
- two '**oy**' words
- two '**ir**' words
- two '**ur**' words.

LANGUAGE STUDY

*Copy these sentences into your book. Change the **verbs** in the brackets to the **present tense**, as shown.*

1 a) The old man (walk) ___walks___ very slowly.

b) He (sit) _____ down on a bench.

c) He (read) _____ the newspaper.

d) The old man (eat) _____ a sandwich.

e) He (feed) _____ the birds.

*Write the sentences again. This time, change the **verbs** to the **past tense**. The first one has been done for you.*

2 a) *The old man walked very slowly.*

*Write the **shortened forms** of these words in your book. The first one has been done for you.*

3 a) did not *didn't*   **b)** I am   **c)** he is

d) we are   **e)** would not   **f)** could not

WRITING WORKSHOP

1 a) I like apples bananas grapes and melons.

b) The dog chased a cat a squirrel a rabbit and a bird.

c) I packed some swimming trunks a bottle of suntan cream a book and my shorts in the case.

d) In my pocket I found a coin two sweet papers and some bubble-gum.

Write out this passage in your book. Write in all the missing punctuation marks.

2 in the middle of the woods it was very quiet there were no sounds except for the birds singing it wasnt time for dinner so the man sat down to rest he tried to sleep but he couldnt

Copy these lists into your book and write in the missing commas.

43

In the biggest, brownest, muddiest river in Africa, two crocodiles lay with their heads just above the water. One of the crocodiles was enormous. The other was not so big.

"Do you know what I would like for my lunch today?" the Enormous Crocodile asked.

"No," the Notsobig One said. "What?"

The Enormous Crocodile grinned, showing hundreds of sharp, white teeth.

"For my lunch today," he said, "I would like a nice juicy little child."

"I never eat children," the Notsobig One said. "Children are too tough and chewy. They are tough and chewy and nasty and bitter."

"Tough and chewy!" cried the Enormous Crocodile. "Nasty and bitter! What awful tommy-rot you talk! They are juicy and yummy! Children are better than fish. You get bigger helpings."

"You are greedy," said the Notsobig One. "You're the greediest croc in the whole river."

Roald Dahl

COMPREHENSION

Write the answers to these questions in your book.

● Starting points ●

1 Which of these words describe the river in Africa: biggest, deepest, widest, brownest, muddiest?

2 What sort of teeth did the Enormous Crocodile have?

3 What did the Enormous Crocodile want to eat for his lunch?

4 Why didn't the Notsobig One like to eat children?

5 Why did the Enormous Crocodile think that children were better to eat than fish?

44

● Moving on ●

Now, answer these questions in your book.

1 Why do you think the crocodiles lay in the water with only their heads just above the surface?

2 Do you like the sound of the Enormous Crocodile? Explain your answer.

3 How do you think the Enormous Crocodile might have caught children?

> *Look at the map. It shows the route I took to get to the town. In the town, I caught children to eat.*

STUDY SKILLS

● Maps and plans ●

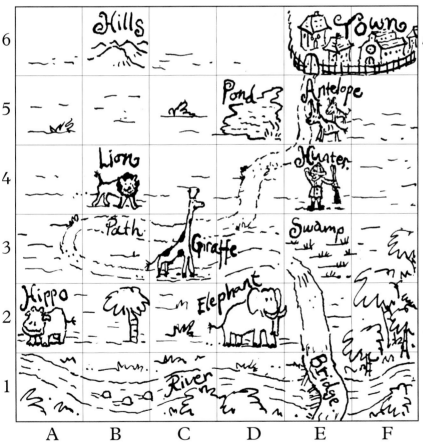

In your book, write what you would find in the following
grid squares:

1 E1	**2** B4	**3** D5	**4** A2
5 B6	**6** E3	**7** F6	**8** E4

> **i** This map has been drawn on a grid of squares. Each **grid square** has a reference letter and number. The elephant is in grid square **D2**.

> **extra**
> *Write a list of the animals the crocodile would have seen on his way to the town. Put them in the order in which he would have passed them.*

WORD STUDY

● Words with an 'eye' sound! ●

*Write these words in your book. Say each one out loud as you copy it down. Underline the part of each word that sounds like '**eye**'. Do it like this:* wh<u>y</u>, hi<u>gh</u>

1 why   2 high   3 cry   4 sigh

5 night   6 try   7 reply   8 fight

9 myself   10 tight   11 rhyme   12 frighten

● 'nce' and 'nge' words ●

*Read the clues below, and then finish each word with either '**nce**' or '**nge**'. Write the completed words in your book.*

1 pri _ _ _   The opposite of princess.

2 ora _ _ _   A colour and a sort of fruit.

3 da _ _ _   You need music to do this!

4 o _ _ _   Something that happens just one time.

5 hi _ _ _ s   Doors have these to help them to open.

6 cha _ _ _   To take a risk.

7 Fra _ _ _   The name of a country.

8 da _ _ _ rous   The opposite of safe.

extra

In your book, write as many words as you can that have the same letter pattern as those listed below:

a) ch<u>ild</u>
b) m<u>ind</u>
c) sm<u>ile</u>.

46

● Comparative adjectives ●

I'm brave.

I'm braver.

I'm the bravest.

We use **comparative adjectives** when we are comparing things.

Copy this chart into your book. Fill in the gaps.

brave	braver	bravest
new	newer	
hard		hardest
	tighter	tightest
	hotter	
warm		
gentle		
	slower	

Look at what happens to **adjectives** ending in a **consonant + 'y'**. e.g. happy – happier – happiest.

● Plurals ●

*Write the **plurals** of these words in your book. (Plural means more than one.)*

1 half   2 fly   3 wolf   4 loaf   5 baby

6 family   7 story   8 pony   9 knife   10 life

11 lorry   12 fairy   13 thief   14 shelf   15 wife

1 Most words ending in '**f** 'or '**fe**' end in '**ves**' in the plural, e.g. half - hal**ves**.

2 Words ending in **consonant + 'y'** end in '**ies**' in the plural, e.g. fl**y** - fl**ies**.

WRITING WORKSHOP

● Exclamation and question marks ●

Copy the sentences below into your book. Fill in the missing **question** *and* **exclamation marks**.

1 Is it safe to cross the road now __

2 Stop __ Don't move __ There's a car coming __

3 Crash __ Bang __ Wallop __

4 What's the matter __

5 You nearly got run over __

● Noise words ●

Print some more noise words in your book. Don't forget to use **exclamation marks**.

● What are they saying? ●

In your book, write what you think each person is saying.

> **i** An **exclamation mark** tells you that the message is important '!' Use an **exclamation mark**:
>
> **1** to give a warning **DANGER!**
>
> **2** to give an order **STOP!**
>
> **3** to show excitement **Yippee! I've won the lottery!**
>
> **4** to show that something hurts **Ouch!**
>
> **5** after a loud noise **BANG!**

> **extra**
>
> *Draw a 'special offer poster' for a shop window. Remember to use* **exclamation marks**.

48

● Nonsense poem ●

Copy and complete this nonsense poem in your book.

If I met a crocodile
I'd run a mile.

If I met a bear
_____.

If I met a goat
_____.

If I met a snake
_____.

extra

Think of some more animals, and then make up some lines about them to add to the end of the poem.

● Write a story - 'How I tricked the crocodile' ●

The crocodile planned to catch you. Write a story that tells how you tricked it instead! Here are some questions that will help you to plan your work.

Where does the story take place?
- in the town?
- in the desert?
- in the jungle?
- somewhere else?

How did you know that the crocodile was trying to catch you?
- Did a monkey tell you?
- Did you overhear the crocodile's plans?

How did you trick the crocodile?
- Did you dig a hole for it to fall into?
- Did you catch it in a net?
- Did you wait until it was asleep to tie it up?

How does your story end?
- Did you make friends with the crocodile?
- Did you punish it?

I'm going to catch a little child to eat.

1 Remember to include in your story the things people said and how they felt.

2 When you have finished your story, check that it makes sense.

Protection

`All creatures need to protect themselves from danger.
They do this in many different ways.

Some animals use their speed to get away from danger. The hare runs very swiftly away from any danger. It has very powerful back legs.

Lots of animals use camouflage to protect themselves. This means that their colours, skin patterns or shapes blend in with their surroundings. The leopard is very hard to see when it is hiding in a tree.

Many animals have strong skin, shells or spikes to protect themselves. The armadillo has a very tough skin. The tortoise has a hard shell to keep it safe. The porcupine is covered with sharp quills.

Some animals use poisons or stings to protect themselves. Some snakes, like the cobra, are poisonous, whilst wasps and bees will sting if they are in danger.

The skunk has a rather nasty weapon. When it is in danger, it turns its back on its attacker and squirts it with an oily liquid which smells awful!

Join the beginning of each sentence to the correct ending. Write the complete sentences in your book.

COMPREHENSION

● Starting points ●

1 A hare has   a smelly liquid.

2 A porcupine is covered   poison to protect itself.

3 A cobra uses   helps it hide in trees.

4 A skunk squirts   powerful back legs.

5 A leopard's skin colour   with sharp quills.

● Moving on ●

Write the names of some other animals that:

1 can run fast when in danger

2 have tough skin

3 are protected by a shell.

STUDY SKILLS

● Analogies ●

Copy and complete these **analogies** *in your book:*

1 Finger is to hand, as toe is to _____ .

2 Day is to week, as _____ is to year.

3 High is to low, as _____ is to down.

4 North is to _____ , as east is to west.

5 Wing is to bird, as fin is to _____.

> ### ℹ️
> Boy is to girl, as man is to woman. When we compare things in this way we call it an **analogy**.

● Using a library ●

Place these books in **alphabetical order**, *according to the first letters of the authors'* **surnames**. *Write them out in a list in your book.*

> *Watership Down by Richard Adams would come first because the author's surname begins with A.*

> ### extra
> Write down the surnames of five children in your class. Rewrite them in **alphabetical order**.

51

WORD STUDY

● Using the suffix 'ful' ●

*Copy this grid into your book. Add the **suffix 'ful'** to each of the **root words** to make some **adjectives**.*

root word ▸	+ suffix 'ful'
power ▸	*powerful*
help ▸	
use ▸	
harm ▸	
care ▸	
hope ▸	
cheer ▸	
joy ▸	
colour ▸	

Whenever we use the **suffix 'ful'** at the end of a word, we really mean 'full of'. 'Powerful' means 'full of power'. Notice that the **suffix 'ful'** only has one 'l'.

I have powerful back legs.

*Use some of the '**ful**' words to fill in the gaps in these sentences. Write the completed sentences in your book.*

1 A rainbow is very _____ .

2 When you cross the road you must be very
   _____ .

3 An electric eel can give a _____ shock.

4 It is _____ to have an umbrella when it rains.

● Using the prefixes 'un' and 'dis' ●

*Give these words **opposite** meanings by adding either '**un**' or '**dis**' to the beginning of each of them. Write the completed words in your book.*

1 ___ do   2 ___ trust   3 ___ pack

4 ___ happy   5 ___ agree   6 ___ appear

7 ___ fair   8 ___ honest

extra

*Instead of adding '**ful**' to the **root words** in the grid, add the **suffix 'less'**. This will give the words the **opposite** meaning. Write them in your book.*

We add **prefixes** to the beginning of some words to change their meaning, e.g. dis + appear = disappear.

LANGUAGE STUDY

● Words that sound the same ●

Choose the correct word from the brackets to finish each sentence. Write out the completed sentences in your book.

1 Can you (hear/here) a car?

2 A butcher sells (meet/meat).

3 I picked the (flour/flower).

4 The castle is over (there/their).

5 Please pass me a (peace/piece) of cake.

extra

Write some sentences in your book which show that you know the difference between the words in each pair.

1 groan, grown
2 hole, whole
3 knight, night
4 aloud, allowed
5 missed, mist
6 sail, sale

● Words that mean the same ●

Write another word that has the same meaning as:

1 unhappy	2 huge	3 little
4 pretty	5 begin	6 foolish
7 angry	8 loud	9 finish

i If you are finding it hard to think of words that have the same meaning, look up each word in a **dictionary**.

Ranjit was <u>sad</u>.

Ranjit was <u>unhappy</u>.

● Words that look the same ●

In your book, write two short sentences for each word to show that it can mean different things. Do it like this:

I ate a date. The date was September 19th.

1 fly	2 fire	3 club	4 ring	5 dear

extra

Write words that mean the same as:

- frightened
- powerful
- modern
- gap
- halt
- imitate

53

WRITING WORKSHOP

● Mixed-up sentences ●

Rewrite these sentences in your book, putting the words in the correct order.

1 A good book is reading Tom.

2 A window broke Yasmin.

3 The ball kicked the footballer.

4 A picture painted the artist.

5 A tent put up the scout.

6 The mouse chased a cat.

I've written some sentences but they don't make sense!

i Always check that what you have written makes sense.

● Silly-animal sentences ●

The words in each column have been mixed up. Choose words from each column to make sensible sentences and write them in your book.

Who?	Does what?	When?
Monkeys	snooze	in the river.
Crocodiles	hang about	in the trees.
Bats	hunt	under the sea.
Lions	swim	under their shells.
Tortoises	eat bananas	upside down.
Foxes	glide around	in the shade.
Sharks	hide	in the forest.

extra

In your book, make up another chart like this about people.

● Labelling and describing ●

The labels which describe the parts of the Tyrannosaurus Rex need to be put in the correct places. Work out where the labels go and write the answers in your book like this:

1 sharp teeth for ripping and tearing

sharp claws for attack

short front legs

sharp teeth for ripping and tearing

powerful hind legs that helped it to stand upright

thick skin

long tail used for attack and defence

Now, use the information you have to write a description of a Tyrannosaurus Rex in your book.

extra

Find out some facts about other dinosaurs. Write some notes about how they protected themselves.

The soup stone

Narrator: Once upon a time there was a poor, homeless man. He had no money for food. One day he had an idea. He picked up a smooth stone and knocked at someone's door.

Woman: Good morning. What's that you've got?

Man: It's a soup stone.

Woman: I've never heard of one of those before. Does it make good soup?

Man: If you let me come in, I'll show you.

Narrator: So the woman took the man into the kitchen and gave him a pan and some water. The man put the stone into the pan, put the pan on to the fire and waited for it to boil.

Man: It's going to be the best soup that you've ever tasted. Have you got such a thing as a carrot? I think that a carrot would really improve the soup.

Narrator: The woman put a carrot into the soup.

Man: Have you got an onion by any chance? I'm sure that it would bring out the flavour of the soup.

Narrator: The woman got an onion and put it into the soup.

Man: It just needs a chicken and some salt and pepper to finish it.

Narrator: The woman put these things in the pan. The smell was delicious. An hour later, the man served the soup.

Woman: This is marvellous. I wish I had a soup stone like yours!

Man: As you've been so kind to me, you can have mine as a special gift.

Narrator: The woman held the stone tightly as she waved goodbye to the man. When the poor man felt hungry again the next day, do you know what he did?

COMPREHENSION

● Starting points ●

Read 'The soup stone' again. Then, complete these sentences in your book.

1 The man was...

2 He picked up a...

3 The man told the woman he had a...

4 The first vegetable the man asked for was a...

5 The man gave the stone to the woman as a...

● Moving on ●

1 What did you think of the man? Why?

2 What did you think of the woman? Why?

3 What do you think the man did when he felt hungry the next day?

extra

Write about a trick you have played on someone.

STUDY SKILLS

● The daily cycle ●

Copy this cycle, which shows the parts of the day, into your book. Think of some of the things you do at each time of day. Write them in your book like this:

In the morning I get up, get dressed, have my breakfast and clean my teeth.

Some things always happen in the same order. We call this a **cycle**.

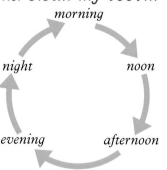

morning

noon

afternoon

evening

night

● A weekly cycle ●

Now draw a weekly cycle, which shows every day of the week. Underneath, list one thing you do on each day.

WORD STUDY

● Syllables ●

i Longer words are made up of separate parts, called **syllables**. When we say words slowly we can hear the separate parts: in + side = inside.

Divide these words into **syllables**. *Write them in your book like this:* *inside = in / side.*

1 inside   **2** garden   **3** pencil   **4** magnet

5 homeless   **6** improve   **7** walking   **8** goodbye

Sometimes we don't say words in the same way that they are written. Some letters are silent.

● Silent letters – 'k' and 'w' ●

Copy these words into your book. Fill in the gaps with either '**k**' *or* '**w**'.

1 _ nock   **2** _ rite   **3** _ now   **4** _ not   **5** _ rap

6 _ nob   **7** _ rong   **8** _ rist   **9** _ riggle   **10** _ nee

Use some of the **silent 'k'** *and* **silent 'w'** *words in the sentences below. Write the completed sentences in your book.*

1 The opposite of right is _____ .

2 A _____ is something you tie with string.

3 You use paper to _____ a parcel.

4 Your _____ is part of your arm.

5 You _____ on a door to let someone know you are there.

extra

*How many words can you think of that have a silent '***b***' in them, like 'com***b***'? Write them in your book.*

LANGUAGE STUDY

● Prepositions ●

*Copy these sentences into your book. Use a **preposition** from the box to fill in the gap in each one.*

1 The man knocked _____ the door.

2 The woman showed him _____ the kitchen.

3 The man took a stone _____ his pocket.

4 He heated a pan of water _____ the fire.

5 When the soup was ready, he took the pan _____ the fire.

i A **preposition** is a place word. It tells you the position of things.

> from
>
> on
>
> into
>
> off
>
> over

● Similes ●

*Think of a word to finish each **simile**. Write the completed **similes** in your book.*

1 As cold as *ice*   2 As strong as a _____

3 As slow as a _____   4 As hairy as a _____

5 As quiet as a _____   6 As tall as a _____

7 As green as _____   8 As sweet as _____

i When we compare things we often use **similes**.

That man tricked me. He was as crafty as a fox.

I ate too much soup. I was as greedy as a pig!

extra

*Finish these **similes** with suitable **adjectives**:*
1 As _____ as a monkey
2 As _____ as a bee
3 As _____ as an elephant
4 As _____ as a kitten.

WRITING WORKSHOP

● Subjects of sentences ●

In your book, complete these sentences using suitable **subjects**.

1 _____ eat grass and give us milk.

2 _____ is a big city.

3 _____ can sing well.

4 _____ is my favourite television programme.

5 _____ was a famous king of England.

6 _____ took an X-ray of my leg.

> **i** Every sentence has a **subject**. The **subject** is the main person or idea in the sentence. The **subject** is usually found just in front of the **verb**:
>
> (**subject**) (**verb**)
>
> <u>Vaheem</u> <u>smiled</u> happily at his present.

● Subjects and predicates ●

Here are the **subjects** *of some sentences. Finish the sentences with suitable* **predicates** *(endings). Write the completed sentences in your book.*

1 The fierce dragon _____ .

2 The huge giant _____ .

3 Cinderella _____ .

4 The wicked witch _____ .

5 The brave knight _____ .

6 Red Riding Hood _____ .

> **i** If you take away the subject from a sentence, the **predicate** is what is left.

60

● What are they saying? ●

Write what you think the people in these pictures are saying. Do it like this:

1 *Come on, Ben! You're nearly there!*

● Writing a conversation ●

Write a conversation that Red Riding Hood might have had with the wolf. Start it like this:

Red Riding Hood: Oh grandmother! What big ears you've got!

Wolf: All the better to hear you with, my dear!

extra

Write the answers to these questions in your book. What sort of things do:

- ***teachers*** *say when there is too much noise?*

- ***parents*** *say when they think your bedroom's untidy?*

- ***friends*** *say when you want to play and they won't let you?*

61

Do you remember?

STUDY SKILLS

*Write the names of these authors in **alphabetical order** according to their surnames:*

1 John Tully   Barbara Mitchelhill

   Jill Jones   Hugh Lofting

   Mike Ratnett   Ted Hughes

These instructions for crossing the road are in the wrong order.

2 Look carefully around for traffic and listen.

   Find a safe place to cross the road.

   Keep looking and listening while you are walking.

   Stand still on the pavement near the kerb before crossing.

   Try not to cross the road near parked cars.

   When nothing is coming, walk quickly across the road.

> Find a safe place to cross the road.
>
> ⬇
>
> Try not to cross the road near parked cars.
>
> ⬇

Write them out correctly as a flow diagram, like this.

WORD STUDY

*Divide these words into **syllables**. Write them in your book like this:*

   inside = in/side

1 **a)** outside   **b)** indoors   **c)** somehow   **d)** airport

   e) until   **f)** magnet   **g)** tablet   **h)** comic

Use the grid to answer the questions.

4	knock	high	happy	dance
3	wrap	colour	myself	write
2	change	sky	chance	knee
1	bedroom	appear	help	strange
	A	**B**	**C**	**D**

2 a) Write the grid square and word that rhymes with 'sky'.

b) Write the words in D2, A4, D3 and A3. Underline the silent letter in each word.

c) Write the grid square and word that rhymes with 'change'.

d) Add 'un' to the beginning of the word in C4.

e) Add 'dis' to the beginning of the word in B1.

f) Add 'ful' to the end of the words in C1 and B3.

g) Write the grid square and word that rhymes with 'dance'.

h) Write down the words in A1 and C3. Write what you notice about them.

LANGUAGE STUDY

1 a) families **b)** wolves **c)** loaves **d)** babies
e) lorries **f)** thieves **g)** halves **h)** flies

2 a) small **b)** quiet **c)** sad **d)** silly
e) strong **f)** fix **g)** talk **h)** nasty

Write down the singular of these words

Write another word that means the same as each of these.

*Finish these **similes** with suitable words.*

3 a) as fast as a _____ **b)** as dry as a _____

c) as sweet as a _____ **d)** as busy as a _____

Write some sentences to show you know the difference between these pairs of words:

4 a) hear/here **b)** there/their **c)** herd/heard

d) meat/meet **e)** pair/pear **f)** threw/through

WRITING WORKSHOP

*Punctuate these sentences with **exclamation** or **question** marks.*

1 a) What's the time _

b) Stop_ Where do you think you are going_

c) Crash_ Bang_ What was that_

d) Crunch_ Slurp_ Who is making all that noise.

Complete each of these sentences with the correct subject from the box.

2 a) A _____ carries food on a tray.

b) A _____ lives next door.

c) An _____ uses brushes and paints.

d) A _____ makes sure people don't break the rules of the game.

e) A _____ carries a message.

f) A _____ makes furniture.

g) A _____ works in an office.

carpenter

neighbour

referee

secretary

waiter

messenger

artist